THE GLEANER SONG

Also by Song Lin:

In Chinese
City Dwellers (1987)
Vestibule (2000)
A Visit to Dai on a Snowy Night (2015)
Oral Message (2016)

In Translation
Fragments et chants d'adieu (2006)
Murailles et couchants (2007)
Sunday Sparrows (2020)

SONG LIN

THE GLEANER SONG

SELECTED POEMS

Translated from the Chinese by Dong Li

PHONEME
MEDIA

DEEP
VELLUM

DALLAS, TEXAS

Phoneme Media, an imprint of Deep Vellum
3000 Commerce St., Dallas, Texas 75226
deepvellum.org · @deepvellum

Deep Vellum Publishing
3000 Commerce St., Dallas, Texas 75226
deepvellum.org · @deepvellum

Deep Vellum is a 501c3 nonprofit literary arts organization founded in 2013 with the mission to bring the world into conversation through literature.

www.giramondopublishing.com

ISBNs: 978-1-64605-144-1 (paperback) | 978-1-64605-145-8 (ebook)

LIBRARY OF CONGRESS CONTROL NUMBER: 2021944770

Cover image: YVdavyd

PRINTED IN THE UNITED STATES OF AMERICA

To my loved ones
&
In memory of the days and nights on the road

Contents

The World Migrating: On Translating Song Lin
Dong Li

I got to know Song Lin well while at Ledig House for a Translation Lab residency. On a long walk in the countryside of Upstate New York, I saw his eyes light up as a deer leapt from the wild into a wide-open field. As the evening hues shifted farther into the forest, his line of sight followed the deer until it vanished into the night. We talked about the deer, and later he asked me to translate a poem that he had written to record the occasion. This is a curious poet who opens himself to the world around him. His songs migrate from one word to another, from one language to another. The landscape of his travels becomes a map of his poetry, which, in turn, amounts to a sensitive anthropology of our migratory world.

Not unlike his predecessor Bei Dao, whose candid declarations of resistance marked the tenor of the time, themes of politics and exile permeate Song's poetic output. When the Tiananmen event exploded in Beijing, Song led student demonstrations in Shanghai and was imprisoned for almost a year. But unlike many self-claimed "exiled poets," Song has never used imprisonment to his advantage. Instead, what has interested Song is the joy of making art out of words and how poetry can group words and form company. His joy in poetic expression led to his lengthy wanderings through France, Singapore, and Argentina. These heightened his sense of language and its central role in his poetry.

Song has been somewhat neglected in his native language. Political pressure was the unspoken background. During those wandering years, his two formidable titles, *Fragments et chants d'adieu* (*Fragments and Farewell Songs*) and *Murailles et couchants* (*City Walls and Sunset*), appeared in French bilingual editions. He was unable to publish in China then, so he used his editorship with the eminent journal *Jintian* to scout out and publish poets living under difficult circumstances. Since his return to China, he continues to support young poets and champions translation. Unlike many poets who are eager to please Western ears, Song advocates for the classics and for a thorough study of the Chinese language. When dividing lines between different camps of poetry and poets widen, Song is the one not to force cohesion, but to promote tolerance and understanding.

Song's faith in poetry and his generosity toward poets across aesthetic, generational, and national boundaries make him one of the most unusual poets to have emerged in recent Chinese history. His poetry weaves through American, classical Chinese, French, and Latin American traditions. His influences are the modernists, the surrealists, the romantics, the deep imagists, and the objectivists – but what distinguishes Song is his ability to take them all, and make them his own, and make them new. His is a lyric that continues to open up horizons.

—*Dong Li*

The Gleaner Song

一

被放逐的时间像永远不能
返回故土的麻风病人，在悬崖下，
在星光的刺下，吐着泡沫。

1

Like a leper who can never return home,
exiled time throws up its white foam
under the cliff, in the thorns of starlight.

采撷者之诗

1

用山鹑的方言呼唤着跑出房子
蓝浆果里的声音我还能听见
雷达站，木轮车，童年的山冈
整个夏天我们都在寻找
坡地开阔而平缓，死者的瓮
半埋着。荒凉的词，仿佛涂上了蜜
我们的乐园向南倾斜，金丝雀飞去飞来
那时还没有特洛伊，我们总是躺着眺望
村庄，水杉高大，像山海经中的
有外乡来的筑路工留下的斧痕
"他闯祸，必不得其死"，老人们说
而我们笑，躲在咒语中摇晃镜子

冬天拨着火炭，夏天就去后山
采撷，坐在树上等待父亲
廊桥消失了，仿佛被突降的暴雨卷走
这是既没有开始也没有结束的地方
人们只是绕着那几棵水杉树走
在历法中生活。狐狸尖叫，大雾
追着我们跑。长途车从海边爬上来
没有父亲，我们踢着小石子回家
夜里我梦遗了。哟，大捧的浆果

The Gleaner Song

1

Calling out in a partridge's dialect while running out of the house,
I could hear a voice in the blueberries:
radar station, wooden carriage, childhood hillocks
that we had been looking for all summer.
The slopes open and smooth, the urn of the dead
half buried. Bleak words, as if dipped in honey.
Our paradise slanted to the south, the canaries flying about.
There was no Troy then, we always lay down and watched
the village, the tall fir tree, like in *Classics of Mountains and Seas*.
There were ax marks left by the construction workers from
          another town.
"No good end for a troublemaker," the elderly said
and we laughed, hiding in the curse, flashing a mirror.

I flicked embers in winter and went to the mountains in summer,
gleaning, sat in the tree waiting for Father.
The bridge disappeared, as if washed away by a summer storm.
This was a place with no beginning nor end.
People just walked around a few fir trees
and lived in their calendars. A fox screeched, a heavy fog
chased after us. A long-distance bus climbed up from the seaside.
Without Father, we kicked broken rocks around and came home.
At night I had a wet dream. Ah, armfuls of berries.

记得吗？那两个发亮的音节，
把我们变成蓝鬼。甚至风也变蓝了
野孩子唱道："雷达兵，天上的雷达兵"
直到中秋的月亮升起，木轮车滑下去
浆果碎了，像伤口流出的血，仿佛为了
让我日后的手稿点染上那种蓝

Do you remember? Those two bright syllables
turned us into blue ghosts. Even the wind blued
a wild children's song: "radar soldier, radar soldier from the sky"
until the moon rose in midautumn, the wooden carriage slid,
berries crushed, as if blood from a wound, as if to dye
my manuscripts so they read with that kind of blue.

Note: "flashing a mirror" is a mythological way of casting light on
disguised evil, turning it back to its original shape, and killing it
with the light. "Those two bright syllables" refers to the Chinese
word for blueberry (蓝莓lánméi).

2

蒙德格伊街。儿子惊呼:" Myrtille "
新上市的浆果摆在货架上。恋人抱吻
晒成棕色的皮肤散发着海藻的气味
假期已结束。地中海留给了墓园守望人
我们避开沙滩营帐,为兽迹所吸引
迷失于山毛榉林中。我想去触摸
高地上的赛壬石,最终表明
那冲动是虚妄的,她或许死于雪崩
像树上的娃娃鱼。而传说活在舌尖

我们都喜欢这南部山区的夏季
村道垂直在门前,花荫遮住窗台
去湖边散步的人回来了
拿着新采的野菊。群峰渐次明亮
畜水池含情脉脉,屋顶更柔和
倒影中的停云像洗衣妇回眸的样子
对山,牛铃丁丁。儿子蹲在灌木丛中
四岁之夏,不知道中文名字的来由
他吃 Myrtille这个词,抬头看见
滑翔机像风筝,轻轻越过瀑布

我的头晕症消失了,字典带来
新的苦恼。我们元素中的土生长着
同样的植物,那些枝条本是为了

2

Rue Montorgueil. My son exclaimed: "Blueberry!"
Fresh berries were on the shelves. Lovers kissed and embraced.
Tanned skins emitted a smell of seaweed.
Vacation was already over. The Mediterranean left to the
        grave watchmen.
We avoided beach tents and were drawn by animal tracks
and got lost in the beech forest. I wanted to touch
the siren rock on the high ground but eventually
the urge was false, perhaps she died in an avalanche of snow
like the giant salamander in the tree. And legend lived on the tip of
        the tongue.

We all liked summer in the southern mountains.
Country paths lay vertically by our doorsteps, flowers shaded the balcony.
Those who went for a walk by the lake came back
with freshly picked wild chrysanthemums. Mountain peaks lit one
        by one,
the reservoir tender with feelings, the roof ever softer, the
        lingering clouds
in the water's reflection looked like a washing woman turning around
in the opposite mountains, cattle bells resounded. My son squatted
in the shrubbery, his summer at the age of four, not knowing
the origin of his Chinese name, he ate the word blueberry and looked up
and saw a glider, like a kite, which swiftly passed the waterfalls.

My headache was gone, the dictionary brought in
new trouble. In the earth of our bodily elements
the same plants grew, whose branches were there

纪念死者。当我们带回的自制果浆
早餐时涂上乡村面包，我将用什么解释
乌饭与寒食，以及丧失的祭天之礼？
一种凝聚的寂静深入到这里
柔软、微热的泥土，款待着我
今天我们又去登山，但选择了另一条路

for the dead. When we put out the homemade jam that we spread
on the country bread at breakfast, how could we explain
black rice and *cold food*, and the lost rituals of worshipping the gods
   of heaven?
A concentrated quietude deepened
into the soft and barely warm earth and served me.
Today we were to climb the mountain but chose another path.

无 题

一枝连翘上
秋天痉挛
异乡人走过河岸
回忆使他变成一个灵魂
高大的秋天，一阵风
把落叶的黄金播入了阁楼
你的夜晚与某个天使搏斗
直到星星变成骨头

白昼之钟赤裸着
一个推迟的约会将你召唤
于是你穿过广场
松树之蓝环绕着古塔
鸟疾飞时
水上写着禁止：
石头的面容闪耀谦逊
痛苦的青苔
无语之舌

Untitled

on a forsythia
autumn shudders
a stranger walks past the river bank
reminiscence turns him into a ghost
towering autumn, a gust of wind
tosses leaf-gold into the garret
your evening battles with a certain angel
until stars become bones

the clock of day naked
a belated meeting beckons
so you cross the square
blue of pine trees around ancient pagodas
birds in flight
no written on the water:
modesty glows on the face of stone
lichen in pain
wordless tongue

遗 忘

1

日晕。头颅。谁退藏于密？
谁的仪表画出虚妄的圆弧？
你眼睛的祭坛深陷着
在未来某个庞大建筑的对面

彗星落向木樨地时
倘若我是你，你或许就是他：一个尾数
她最后的回首穿过了
呦呦鹿鸣

Forgetting

1

The sundial   heads   that receded in secret.
Whose meter drew out their false curves?
The altar of your eyes was sunken,
facing an immense building of tomorrow.

When a comet hit Muxidi.
If I were you, you could be him: a mantissa,
her last glance crossed
the bellowing of the deer.

Note: Muxidi was an important access point into central Beijing
from the west suburbs. On June 4, 1989, the greatest number of
casualties occurred here.

2

雪的谐音喷涌
花，无痛地绽放
一朵催开了死亡的非花
是真的。它攀上了你的名字

痉挛的灌木下
道具般的脚趾涂着萤火虫的黑盐
也是这么被抬走了
像极了新近地震中的场面

2

The red homonym of snow, spewing
flowers, blooming painlessly.
A flower triggered the opening nonflower of death
which was real. It climbed onto your name

under shrubs in spasm –
prop-like toes were painted in the black salt of fireflies
and were carried away like this,
very much like the scenes of the recent earthquake.

3

喷枪那闪电节奏的火舌
吻遍娇嫩的脸。清晨的水龙头
把夜的灰烬灌溉了又灌溉
结痂的将长成石笋，在心脏部位

一个失踪者走来，一个失踪太久的
失踪者，瘦长的手臂像唐·吉诃德
读秒的时间到了。你来读，像秒针一样读
履带的嘎嘎声里是什么已对峙了千年？

3

Lightning-fast flames from the machine guns
kissed every tender face. The morning taps
washed over and over night's ashes.
The scabs would turn into stalagmites, in the heart.

A missing person came by, a person missing
for too long, his thin arms looking like Don Quixote's.
Countdown time was up. Please read, read like the second hand of
        the clock
in the rattling of tracks, what has been mired in enmity for a
        thousand years?

蕉城：1970年

苦闷的海峡。台风的最高指示一次次登陆。
高音喇叭取代月亮，向天空宣讲斗争的哲学。
龙眼树像一些瞎子，站在低矮的山冈上，
什么也不指望。螃蟹吐着泡沫，
依旧生活在史前的莽荒中。
疍人的小木屋倚靠着黑暗的滩涂。

我十一岁，长着乡村蛾子的脸，
一头木麻黄的乱发。在一枚捡到的金色
弹壳上吹奏义勇军进行曲和红色少年之歌。
我记得涌向郊外观看行刑的人群，
泄洪般相互踩踏的人群，带着狂喜的表情，
比防空演习更不要命地奔跑着。

我记得那些夏夜，无尽的街头游荡。
有人指控我（当然是向我父母）
为了一部样板戏而翻墙进入了人民剧场
——居然没有买票！大人泼水消暑；
儿童们在巷子里学习怎样"坐飞机"。
我缺乏证据，但我知道
我父母的战友中间，必然有一个告密者。

他穿着运动鞋，像一个矫健的体育老师，
他盯着我，靠近我，突然指甲比蚱蜢更快地弹起，
弹向我额头上忧郁的青春痘。

Jiaocheng, 1970

The strait in anguish. Severe typhoons repeatedly made landfall.
The loudspeaker replaced the moon, preaching to the sky the philosophy
        of war.
The longan trees, like the blind, stood on the low hillocks,
nothing to look forward to. The crabs blew bubbles,
still living in their prehistoric recklessness.
The cabins of the boat people leaned against dark shoals.

I was eleven, my face a country moth,
dirty-blond hair, matted. On a golden shell casing that I found,
I played the national anthem and the Red Youngsters song.
I remember people streaming to watch executions in the suburb.
Like a flood, the crowd stamped on each other, wild with joy
as if running for life, more frantic than during air-defense exercises.

I remember those summer nights, endless street wanderings.
Someone accused me (of course to my parents)
of sneaking into the People's Theater over the wall to see a model opera
without buying a ticket! Adults splashed water to cool down summer
        heat;
children were learning how to "ride a plane" in the alleyways.
I had no evidence but I knew,
among my parents' comrades, there must have been an informer.

He wore sneakers, like a robust PE teacher.
He stared at me, came closer, his fingernail flicked: faster than
        a grasshopper,
he flicked the melancholy pimple on my forehead.

答 问
—— 给费迎晓

1

所以，小姐，一旦我们问："为什么？"
那延宕着的就变成了质疑。
它就像一柄剑在匣中鸣叫着，虽然
佩剑的人还没诞生。迄今为止
诗歌并未超越那尖锐的声音。

2

我们不过是流星。原初的
沉睡着，有待叩问，但岁月匆匆。
当一行文字迷失于雾中，我们身上的逝者
总会适时回来，愤怒地反驳，
或微笑着为我们指点迷津。

3

写作是一扇门，开向原野，
我们的进出也是太阳每天的升降，
有一种恍惚难以抵达。于是秋天走来，
涂抹体内的色彩，使它深化，
然后消隐，像火狐的一瞥。

Q & A
for Fei Yingxiao

1

So, dear lady, once we ask why,
procrastination turns to questioning,
like a sword shrieking in the scabbard, though
the sword carrier is not yet born. So far,
poetry has not surpassed that shrill sound.

2

We are but meteors. The origins
sleep still, waiting to be questioned, but years are quickly gone.
When a line of words loses itself in fog, the dead in us
always return in time, rebutting in anger
or with a smile marking out the path.

3

Writing is a door that opens to the open field,
we come in and out as the sun rises and sets,
there is a trance, difficult to arrive at. So autumn walks here,
paints its inside and deepens itself,
then vanishes, like the glimpse of a red panda.

4

这些是差异：过去意味着反复，
未来难以预测；面对着面的人，
陷入大洋的沉默。而风在驱体的边缘
卷曲。风摇着我们，像摇着帆，
不知不觉中完成了过渡。

5

所以我们必须警惕身分不明的，
长久失踪的东西，隶属于更大的传统，
在更远的地方移动，遮蔽在光线中 ——
真实，像一只准确无误的杯子，
被突然递到我们面前。

4

These are differences: the past means to repeat,
the future is difficult to predict; face-to-face, we
sink into oceanic silence. Close to the bodily edge, wind
rolls. Wind shakes us, like shaking the sail,
and in no time the crossing is done.

5

So we must watch out for the nameless,
for the long lost, for those who belong to greater traditions
that move at a farther place, who are covered in light –
truth, accurate as glass,
is suddenly handed to us.

《断片与骊歌》节选

一片空白。这只人种志学陶器是残破的，难以再现初始之圆 。
遗嘱的悲哀传给了下一代。

from **Fragments and Farewell Songs**

A field of emptiness. An anthropological pottery is shattered, impossible to return to its early roundness. The sorrow of wills passes into the next generation.

那个被记忆压垮的生者是你，心情沉重。有雾腾起，红色的雾，在海上。护照像失去土地者的地契，被你徒然攥着。行李箱是你的独木舟，在人群中吱吱作响，额头冒着汗，嘴角尝到盐的滋味 。 铁丝网的黑灌木开花了，你这侥幸的人，认识其中的一朵。边界可疑的光晃在你脸上。一种对质。当手从小窗口收回，印戳那制度化的烫伤就烙在皮肤上。你要走了吗？你这像囚徒的人，行李箱里有几页残破的手稿，浮云的遗嘱，家传的护身符。

Crushed by memory, you survive, heart heavy. Fog rises, fog in red, fog on the sea. Like the title deed of a landless owner is the passport that you now clutch in vain. The suitcase is your canoe, creaking through the crowd. Sweat on the forehead. Taste of salt in mouth corners. Black shrubs blossom on barbed wires. You are the lucky one who recognizes one of the flowers. The suspicious light of borders flashes on your face. An enmity. When the hand retreats from the small opening of a window, the systematic burn of the stamp scars the skin. Are you ready to leave, you the prisoner? A few brittle reams of manuscripts, the will of clouds adrift, the amulet of the family.

反向的秋天深入城市，水，从银亮变成了暗红。钓鱼人在防波堤上抽烟，看着上涨的河面，景色中偏暗的部分容易被忽略，码头灰蒙蒙，提前亮起的灯，也把隐蔽的冒险提前。公墓外的探戈在孤独的异乡人眼中仿佛骷髅的死亡之舞；木偶艺人穿着小丑的花衣裳：快乐是他的红鼻子，清白是他的贫穷。雾，弓着猫的腰身过桥。一个行人停下擦拭眼镜，仿佛想擦去突然出现的、对一段往事的内疚。你什么也没变，除了看的方式——固执于眼睛对世界的爱。

Retreating autumn deepens in the city. Water turns from silver to maroon. A fisherman smokes on the bank, looking at the rising tide. The dark tones in the landscape are often overlooked. The bank, gray in the fog. The early-lit lamps drag hidden adventures ahead of their time. In the eyes of a lonely wanderer, the tango outside the cemetery swings to a skeletal dance of death. The puppeteer wears the flashy clothes of a clown: happiness is his red nose and innocence, his poverty. Fog crosses the bridge like a crouching cat. A pedestrian stops to wipe his glasses as if he wants to wipe out his sudden guilt for things long past. You have not changed, except for your ways of looking – the eyes are still stubbornly in love with the world.

星宿和母语，寒冷的光环，
低飞在异乡人的血液里，
像古代进入大山中的徒步者，
相信护身符的驱邪术，你相信
这些字根的龙胆没有死。
在如此众多坚硬的物体表面，
经历着不朽的渴望——藏诸名山，
或沉诸深井，甲骨与简帛
再度显露出来，带着时间、
黏土和身体的擦痕。
镊子的精神是越来越纤细。
吹去尘土。此乃初始的天问：
作《易》者其有忧患乎？
那位大师把一一数过的蓍草
敷在伤口上，如此经过了数千年。
而词语在被烘烤的、脆薄的
舌头上皲裂，犹如河流经过
不断的汇合　，终于到达开阔的
寂静，在遗忘的块状熔渣下面。
无论你在哪，母语的微火
都照彻你的睡眠，陪伴着你，
在冻土带去接近一座冰山。
指南车旋转时，苍颉飞过。

Stars and mother tongues, cold auras
fly low in the blood of a stranger.
Like ancient walkers who go to the mountains
and believe in the magic exorcism of amulets, you believe
that the gentian of the roots of words has not died.
On the hard surface of things
an immortal longing takes place – hidden in famous mountains
or sinking in deep wells, oracles as well as bamboo and silk scripts
reveal themselves again, with time,
clay, and scratches on the body.
The spirit of the tweezers becomes more and more slender.
Dust blown away. This is the first Heavenly Question:
did the writer of *I Ching* have worldly worries?
The master counted the yarrows and applied them
to the wounds. Thus thousands of years are gone.
Words break on the baked
brittle tongue – as rivers
come together before the emergence
of that vast stillness, lying forgotten under the slagheaps.
Wherever you are, the pale fire of mother tongues
lights through sleep and is with you
as you get closer to an iceberg in the tundra.
When the south-pointing chariot turns, Cangjie flies over.

Note: Cangjie is claimed to be the inventor of Chinese characters.

九十岁的祖母坐着，肘搁在桌布上。窗外，海暗下来，比铅还重。光逃散，巨浪几乎压住屋顶。这时你想，诗，终不可取代面包，或在垃圾堆上面重建游乐场。油污只能一点点排除。你出去，走向一截旧城墙。

The ninety-year-old grandmother sits, elbows on the tablecloth. Outside the window the sea dims, heavier than lead. Light flees. Massive waves almost press on the roof. Then you think, poetry won't replace bread or build an amusement park over a garbage dump. Oil stains can only be wiped out, bit by bit. You go out, toward a fragment of the ancient city wall.

动物的眼睛里总是漫溢着使人想到乡愁的物质，不依赖于任何
发出声音的语言。河，向下，清凉涨满我的肺，为了喝到水身
体必须前倾着跪下来，从前在故乡的山中也是这么跪着。

倒影中一张晃动的脸注视你，
手浸入时被什么打碎了，
但你更强烈地感觉到了它。
记忆是另一种汹涌。

Always something brimming in the eyes of animals
reminds one of nostalgia, a language independent of any
voice. The river, facedown, a coolness fills my lungs. In
order to drink, one has to kneel forward. I used to kneel
down like this in the mountains of home.

In the reflection a trembling face watches you
and breaks as you dip your hand in the water
but you feel it, the feeling stronger than ever.
Memory is another kind of rage.

这是一封天外来信，
像某个外星人
留在街角的涂鸦，
讲着一个无人知晓的故事。
你自己的故事该怎样去讲述，
如果记忆之瓮
埋在一个无人知晓的地方？
　"父亲，我一直在等你归来，
我一直站在早年的山上
等待你。"总是这样，
完成后的空虚击中了脊椎。
雪中取火，不留足迹，
是困难的，何况肝脑涂地。

This is a letter from elsewhere,
like graffiti around the corner
left by an anonymous alien,
now telling an unknown story.
If the urn of memory
is buried in an unknown place,
how will you tell your own story?
"Father, I have been waiting for your return,
I have been standing on the mountain of our early years,
waiting for you." As always,
an emptiness hits the spine after an ending.
To take fire out of snow, to walk without a trace,
that is difficult, let alone a life laid down in sacrifice.

死亡与赞美（组诗选）

6

博物馆中这些高贵的鹿
身影投映出玻璃器皿的世界
一动不动，而行进着死亡的节奏
昏死的鹿，角枝挑起

进入林中的无边暖夜时
秘密的舞蹈早已向群狼公开
那黄昏般微薄的皮
血的茸毛，蹦跳着，但一动不动

当车队跟随蓝色的火去寻找一个神
逐鹿人平伸的手臂被落日烧伤
鹿，在相互抵消的态度里转身

时间清脆的食物只能由时间消受
昏死两次的鹿激动不已
从骷髅的洞孔中吹出喜悦的风

from **Death and Praise**

6

these noble deer in the museum
whose shadows reflect a glassware world
stay motionless as the fugue marches on
as faintly the deer, antlers forward,

tread into the infinite warm night of the forest
their secret dance reveals itself to a wolf pack
skin thin like twilight
blood downy, bobbing yet motionless

as the motorcade follows blue fire to find a god
the setting sun scorches the deer hunters' stretched arms
the deer turn around in a pose that cancels itself

food still fresh in time can only be consumed by time
the deer that fainted twice are now more than excited
and blow the winds of joy out from skeletal caves

啊！虚无的光点。啊！天使
我这样把你呼唤，日复一日
在林中路上，我看见你潜伏着一只豹
化开，还原，不是一个真实的人

偶然地它挣脱你，完全松弛
在你昏迷的深沉状态里低吼
这被热烈的激情煎熬的豹子
也已昏死过去，失去了挑逗

不仅一只豹在你周围
——座椅旁，手臂间，头发里
瞳孔中心各有一只幼小的

无情地撕裂。当欲望回到你的躯体
带着美的伤痕逃离，你飞过
把我抛在豹子中，一群又一群

17

alas! mottled light of the void – alas! angels
I call you so, day after day
en route to the forest, I see a leopard lurk in you
dissolve and restore itself, not a true being

occasionally it breaks free, entirely at ease
and growls in your deep coma –
the leopard afflicted by burning passion
now faints, without a tease

not only is there a leopard around you
– by the bench, between the arms, in your hair
in each pupil there is also a cub

which tears ruthlessly – when desire returns to your body
and flees with beautiful wounds, you fly over
flinging me onto the leopards, flock after flock –

这是不可避免的失语：一个人，在外邦。啊！"冬天使我们温暖。"这不是不可能的仰视：一个人死后漂过塞纳河。

保罗·策兰畅饮塞纳，越喝越渴。他喝着黑暗，从局部到全部的黑暗；他喝掉最后一个词的词根。

最纯洁的最先赴死。放弃抵抗——你，光荣的逃兵，抛弃了集中营、早年、滑稽的纳粹；你也尽数把耻辱还给了犹太人，让他们继续流浪，挨打，寻求着拯救。

漂啊，从塞纳到约旦，从巴黎到耶路撒冷。保罗·策兰用眼睛喝，用他自己发明的喝法喝，一个人畅饮着来自天国和地狱的两条河。

他的眼睛睁开在我们的眼睛里。他说："当上帝叫我喝时。"

Paul Celan by the Seine

This unavoidable speechlessness: alone, in a foreign land. Alas, "winter warms us." This impossible supineness: a dead man floats over the Seine.

Paul Celan drinks the Seine to his heart's content. The more he drinks, the thirstier he becomes. From partial darkness to the full: he drinks away the root of the last word.

The purest go for death the earliest. Resistance off the map – you, glorious deserter, abandoned the concentration camp, the youth, the laughable Nazis. You returned shame to the witnesses, were exiled still, beaten, sought salvation.

Afloat, from the Seine to Jordan, from Paris to Jerusalem. Paul Celan drinks with his eyes, drinks in his own inventive ways. Alone, he drinks the two rivers from heaven and hell.

His eyes open in our eyes. "When god asks me to drink," he says.

Note: the line "The more he drinks, the thirstier he becomes" is adapted from Arthur Schopenhauer.

马科斯·恩斯特

他教会人们对付恐怖的知识
一个发电站在鸟腹中发电
夜大放光明

十万只鸟把黑暗拦在警界线外
植物的婚礼越来越隆重
而人类没有被邀请
人类在羞耻的睡眠里过河

Max Ernst

he gave people the knowledge to fight terror
a power station generates electricity in a bird's belly
night shines brilliantly

ten thousand birds fence off darkness beyond the cordon
the plants' weddings more lavish than ever
yet humans are not invited
they cross the river in the slumber of shame

走下蒙马特

雾像一场热病。披着霓虹灯
踉跄而行的醉汉，抱住电线杆倾吐衷曲，
仿佛抱着一位天使。
我走下灰色的高地蒙马特。

红磨坊的大风车在巴黎上空倾斜，
啤酒杯溢出泡沫。夜的边缘，
一只猫梦见了达利式超现实绘画：
月亮嗅着侍者盘中浇上香脂的草莓。

狂欢的、必死的肉体摇摆。
萨克斯旋风与塔兰泰拉姐妹，
中魔的水晶鞋旋转不停。
那边，电话亭里，一个女人在嘶喊。

告别了一次异乡人的感伤聚会，
我要睡觉！让酒这个绿色幽人陪我结束
游荡的一夜，大汗淋漓的一夜。
我走下灰色的高地蒙马特。

告诉我，垃圾中翻捡的老人，
在哪条街，哪个流光溢彩的路口旁，
我又看见了你，波德莱尔诗中的人物，
你空洞的一瞥能把世界毁灭？

A Walk Down Montmartre

Fog feels like a fever. Under neon lights
a stumbling drunkard holds an electric post
as if holding an angel, pouring out his heart.
I walk down the gray hill of Montmartre.

The windmill of Moulin Rouge slants on the Paris sky,
beer glasses brim with foam. By night's edge,
a cat dreams of a Daliesque painting:
the moon sniffs at strawberries and cream on the serving plate.

The carnivalistic fatal swing of the flesh.
Whirlwinds of saxophone and Tarantella sisters,
crystal shoes on a spell endlessly spin.
There in the telephone booth, a lady cries out.

After a sad expatriate party,
I want to sleep! Let absinthe, this green gloomy spirit,
escort me till the end of a night adrift, a drenched night.
I walk down the gray hill of Montmartre.

Tell me, old man gleaning in the trash,
on which street, around which glittering corner,
do I see you again, a figure from the verse of Baudelaire,
whose empty glance would destroy the world?

布洛涅林中

湖水的碎银，在巴黎的左侧
狮子座越过火圈。

松针，你的仪式道具。

风数你变灰的头发，
睫毛，影子凌乱的狂草。

桨，沉默之臂划过蓝天
兜着圈子，干燥像孩童挖掘的沙井
在梦之岸坍塌下来。
呼吸与风交替着
串串水珠的松林夕照
挂上隐居者的阁楼。

巨人头颅，无人授受
磨亮渡口的老钟远在西岱岛，
敲打死囚的回忆。

火鹤，你渴慕的竖琴，
弹拨湖心。
彩虹里盲目的金子挥霍着，
覆盆子的受难日，
林妖现身于马戏团，
爻辞之梅酸涩，
没有归期。

Bois de Boulogne

scattered lake's silver, west of Paris
Leo jumps through a fire hoop

pine needles, your ritual props

wind fingers your graying hair
eyelashes, wild grass of unkempt shadows

an oar, a silent arm that slices the sky
draws out loops, arid like a sandbox dug up by children
now falling apart by the dream shore
breath intersects wind
clusters of water droplets in the pine-forest twilight
hang onto the garret of a recluse

a giant's head, no one accepts
the old clock far on the Île de la Cité varnishes the ferry
and unlocks the memory of death row inmates

dear flamingo, the lyre that you pine for
plucks the lake's heart
in the rainbow, blind gold is blown away
Good Friday of raspberries
Wood Demon appears in the circus
I Ching's six-line statements of bitter sour plums
no date of return

从水圈到水圈，
星的王冠被夜叉击碎。

铁塔下边走来一个亡命者。

from water loop to water loop
crown of stars smashed by the night witch

from under the iron tower a fugitive arrives

马 戏

1

面前这朵欺人的云，
像女骑师红色的头发，
或探头探脑的人
看见它的样子。

2

如此这般吹着口哨，
把美女切穿，肢解，
从丝绸里取出僵硬的残躯，
没有血滴下，没有恐惧；
下凡的天使，彩翼着火，
和自己互博，忙于自救。
人人都忙于自救。
不知不觉中角色替换。

3

杂耍。风。帽子旋舞，
帽子掉到地上，他不得不弯下腰。

The Circus

1

a sly cloud before the eyes
mimics a horsewoman's red hair
or how a sneaky person
reacts upon seeing it

2

whistle a little tune
cut through a beauty, dismember her
take out stiff flesh from silk
no blood drips, no fear
an earth angel, colored wings on fire
fights with herself, fighting to save herself
everybody is fighting to save himself
roles change in no time

3

acrobatics. wind. a hat spins
and drops on the ground, he has to bend

4

一柄剑正缓缓穿过咽喉，
一柄悬而未决的剑，
太多的目光将它粉碎。

5

腾挪，升空，一展身手的时候到了。
在标杠上他意识到，
人不过是猿猴中的一种。
你呢？如果你是天使，
你是否总是从穹顶的高度瞻眺，
说悲愁是技艺。

6

弥漫的，零度的夜，
词语的抹香鲸返回海底。
现在他是一座岛，孤高的
钢丝索的现象学，
他也是他自己的搭挡，
靶子与飞镖，
名叫尤利西斯的狗，
鼻子冰凉。

4

a sword pierces through a throat
a sword in suspense
too much attention smashes it to dust

5

swing, rise, time to show off
on the bar he realizes
human is but a kind of ape
and you? if you are an angel
do you always watch from the vault
and say sorrow is craft

6

diffuse night, degree zero
the sperm whale of words returns to the seabed
now he is an island, lonesome
phenomenology on the steel cable
he is his own partner in crime
dart and board
a god named Ulysses
nose ice-cold

7

自行车上
十个人搭起一堵人墙，
肌肉的迭韵，高耸入云；
十个人变成一只孔雀，
旋转着，支撑着，
几乎做到了——
一只赤裸的孔雀。

8

把火喷向围观者，
点燃虚空，
与星星成为一体，
或像陨石滚过地毯的寂静。

9

这是技艺，诗的翅膀，
不超过躯体
或躯体笨拙的运动。
但在极限的努力中二者相似，
诗与人的蛙跳，
不超过一点点惊讶的距离，

当天使的秋千荡过。

7

on the bike
ten people make themselves into a wall
muscles rhyme and tower into clouds
ten people turn themselves into a peacock
spin and hold on
as if they made it –
into a naked peacock

8

fire blown toward the audience
lights up the void
becomes one with the stars
or as still as if a meteor had rolled onto a carpet

9

this is craft, wings of poetry
a sport that surpasses
no physique or its clumsiness
in their extreme effort they mirror each other
poetry and a person's frog jump
no trespassing the distance of surprise

when the angel's swing swings by

10

她把马群称作波状的时间，
鞭打，驱策，点名，
一圈又一圈，闪闪发光。
在它们中间她就像一个威严的女王。
虽然她终不能驯服
那匹混合、怪诞、
最后的人马。

10

she calls the herd of horses the rippling time
whip, shoo, roll call
a round after a round, glittering
among them she resembles a dignified queen
though she could never tame
that hybrid that absurd
last centaur

临 近

酒的乡愁。一支歌。无所事事烦闷的回忆。是什么隔离了我与遥远？蓦然回首中漂浮的是归乡之路的幻影吗？鹤，飞越虚空的冰。

如果故园不野蛮，异乡不会有更多漫游者。但我们不知道天气的阴晦原本来自万古愁的遗传。过去即未来。我们种姓象征中的巨龙在贪欲喧嚣声中被更大的贪欲所驯服。麒麟的独角、凤凰的美冠早已随崩溃的礼乐灰飞烟灭了。世界贫血地凸现在它那火山与洪水的双重影像中，废墟裸露末日之美。

诗人，将你遭放逐的声音注入遗忘的颅腔，既不太迟，也不太早。"解放"是对被缚者最原始的祝福。除非用酒温暖骨头，我们以泪水为粮食的日子还嫌不够悠长？酒跳出鹤的机舱，为我们打开落向无地的降落伞。

悬而未决从日子那边向我们临近了，星空与恐惧临近了。我在一个停顿与下一个停顿之间，如被光芒扔在遗忘之河上的浮标。远离，克制，活着就是与死亡对饮。

Near

Homesick of wine. A song. Ennui, anguished
reminiscence. What separates me from the faraway?
Looking back on a whim, is it a mirage of the way home
that wavers in the mind? Crane, the ice that flies through
the void.

Should our homeland be not barbaric, there would
be no more wanderers. This dim weather, unknown to
us, inherits sorrows from long-gone forevers. The past
is the future. In the noise of greed, the giant dragon that
symbolizes our race becomes tamed by ever-greater greed.
The unicorn horn, the phoenix crown have long vanished
into thin smoke as music and mores crumbled to ashes.
The world bloodlessly emerges in the double image of
volcano and flood, as ruins expose the beauty of doomsday.

Dear poet, pour your exiled voice into the long-
forgotten cranial cavity, not too late, nor too early.
"Liberation," an ancient blessing for the oppressed.
Unless we warm our bones with wine, aren't the days
unbearably long when we take tears for food? Wine jumps
from the crane's cabin and opens for us a parachute to the
groundless void.

From the days, dangling, now nears us, starry sky
and terror near. I stand between this break and the next
breaking, as if a buoy left on the river by light. Separation,
restraint, living is to drink with death.

漂泊状态的隐喻

十二座一模一样的桥上，
没有哪一座不是车水马龙。

晚钟震响，众鸟敛迹，
尖顶隐入灰暗的天空。

目光茫然，风中最后的树叶
颤抖着，不知落向何处。

强烈感觉到分裂的自我，
仿佛十二座桥上都站着你。

听着风中的赞美诗，
置身于一片熊熊火海。

那时大雪的伞兵还在集结，
灵魂的飞蛾已劈开教堂的烛焰，

炽然超升，成为空气与黑暗。
风在桥上哭喊。那是谁的灵魂？

成为你自己，而不是别人的灵魂，
星星一样寒冷，孤独。

在车辆的尘嚣和肉体的庆典中，
成为河流，带走无言的哀愁。

Metaphor of the Floating Life

On the twelve identical bridges
not a single one without endless streams of traffic.

The evening bell tolled, birds retrieved their shadows,
steeples faded into a gray sky.

Eyes in a daze, last leaves in the wind
kept trembling, not knowing where to fall.

A spurt of feelings from the divided self
as if you stood on every one of the twelve bridges.

Listening to praise songs on the wind
you were in an ocean of raging fire.

Paratroopers of the heavy snow still gathering then,
the moths of the soul chopped open the church's candlelight.

Rising up intensely, they became air and darkness.
The wind cried out on the bridge, whose soul was that?

Become yourself, not the soul of another person,
cold and lonely like stars.

In the bustle of traffic and celebration of the flesh,
become a river, washing away silent sorrows.

塔上的圣人又怎样了呢？
空空的眼睛望入宇宙。

他脚边的怪兽那耷拉下的翅膀，
遮住了瞬间的天堂和地狱。

漂泊的雪覆盖漂泊者的大地，
树的疤痕，你自我的印迹，多么刺目。

What about the saint in the pagoda?
Hollowed eyes saw into the universe.

Drooping wings of the little monster by his feet
covered heaven and hell in a flash.

Floating snow blanketed the land of the wanderers,
tree scars, your own traces, so glaring, and glaring.

2

你闯入，你这携带着死亡
胎记的漂泊者。醒来，
镜子映出一个倒数的日期。

2

You break in, you the drifter who carries
the birthmark of death. When you wake,
the mirror reflects a date, reversed.

博尔赫斯对中国的想象

沙漏。秒。最细腻的皮肤的触觉。
玉如意。痒。你读过的书中
既无页码又无标点的秘籍。
太阳的章节。月亮的章节。海的章节。
哑剧的脚本。一首比枝形吊灯更美的
佚名作者的回文诗那循环的织锦。
宫女在奉献之夜对皇帝的规劝。
《尔雅》的一个章节或《易经》的一个对卦。
大禹的病足和铁鞋。滔滔江河。
徒步丈量世界的、作为K的原型的竖亥。
（卡夫卡知道，他永远到不了极地）。
函古关的两扇门，桌上摆着那
字迹未干的《道德经》的第一个版本。
空虚的富足。逝去的回归。
南海鲛人的一滴变成珍珠的眼泪。
李商隐写给某个女道士的无题诗。
爬上泰山的一只阿根廷蚂蚁。
鉴真号水手划船时整齐的动作。
一张利马窦在肇庆绘制的坤舆图。
宇宙飞船上看到的万里长城。
象征天圆地方的一枚古钱币。
雪落在永乐大钟上发出的声音。
江南那东方威尼斯的富庶与颓废。
考古学家的镊子。木偶的提线。
《山海经》里闻所未闻的奇异动物。
兵马俑的沉默。丹客的炉与剑。
我在日本的一块石碑前

Jorge Luis Borges Imagines China

A sandglass. A second. Touch of the finest skin.
Jade of joy. An itch. Secrets in books you have read
sans a page number sans a punctuation mark.
Chapter of the sun. Chapter of the moon. Chapter of the sea.
A pantomime script. A palindrome poem by an anonymous
author more beautiful than a chandelier, a rotating brocade.
A lady-in-waiting advising the emperor on Night of Devotion.
A chapter from *Erya* or a hexagram couplet from *I Ching*.
Wounded feet and iron shoes of Yu the Great. Waters rushing.
Shu Hai walks barefoot to measure the world, as prototype of K.
(Kafka knows he will never reach the two poles.)
Two gates to Hangu Pass, on the table sits
the first version of *Tao Te Ching*, ink still wet.
Affluent vacuity. Return of disappearance.
A tear from an ancient mermaid drips into a pearl.
Li Shangyin writes an untitled poem to some Daoist lady.
An Argentinian ant climbs up Mount Tai.
Sailors row in unison on Jianzhen's boat.
Matteo Ricci draws in Zhaoqing the *Map of the World's Kingdoms.*
The Great Wall of China seen from a spacecraft.
An ancient coin symbolizes round sky square earth.
The sound of snow falling on the Grand Bell of Yongle.
The opulence and decadence of oriental Venice in South-of-Yangtze.
Archaeologists' tweezers. Puppets' pulling strings.
Unheard-of mysterious creatures in *Classics of Mountains and Seas*.
Silence of Terracotta Army. Furnace and sword of the Chinese alchemists.
Before a stele in Japan I read through the palms

用手掌阅读过的天朝的不朽铭文。
与布宜诺斯艾利斯的一个铜门环对应的
上海石库门上的另一个铜门环。

of my hands the immortal inscriptions of the Middle Kingdom.
A bronze doorknob in Buenos Aires calls out to
another bronze doorknob in a Shikumen from Shanghai.

迷 楼

　　　　观音山上，老人指点一处禅院，称此
　　　　地曾是隋炀帝迷楼旧址，因有感。

镜中，俯仰的螺钿乱抖，
嬉笑又追逐，取悦着皇帝。
曲房密室洞开仿真的花烛夜。

如果献上金枝和玉兽的人，
只为一睹运河上缓缓驶来的御船，
又何必惊异于宫苑深处的流萤？

他老了，身体的拱桥涨满
欲望源源无尽的春水，
他抽空自己，在庞大帝国的羞处。

恨不能把天下都装进这门牖之中，
又恐怕大限已近，游廊太短，
且琼花那勾魂的美也可索命。

镜子吐出的弑者占据了四野。
他怕的其实是自己，从某个轮回中，
将脖子套向锦带，茫然竦惕。

Tower of Enchantment

On Mount Guanyin an elder points to a Buddhist temple, saying this is the site of Emperor Yang of Sui's Tower of Enchantment, thus the poem.

in the mirror supine lacquer wares shake unwillingly
laughter and wooing, to please the emperor
music rooms, secret chambers, fling and fake for the wedding night

if one presents gold leaf and a jade beast
to catch a glimpse of the royal boat slow on the Grand Canal
why would fireflies deep in the palace take one aback?

he grows old, the arched bridge of his body brims
with boundless spring waters of desire
he drains himself dry, in the loins of the opulent empire

he's anxious to take the whole world into his lattice window
yet fears that his days are numbered and the corridor too short
the beauty of butterfly flowers captivates with killing charm

the mirror spits out assassins who fill up the fields
what he fears after all is himself, in some reincarnation
neck into a brocade band, soberly at a loss

西湖的晴和雨

塔中的舍利在夜晚放光，在白天
说着箴言：摆渡的人正打开一扇水之门！
曾经是禁苑的内湖泄漏了春色，
馈赠午后一场短暂的晴雨交合。

从波心吹来蚕与蛾的思乡曲，
太阳在云中吐丝，在水面织网，
我在你眼睛里垂钓红鲤鱼，
上岸来呀，快接住这个耀眼的词。

湖畔派坐着痛饮杯中的虹霓，
当风把堤上接踵的游人熏得睡着了，
苏小小就从墓里出来，唱一曲：
云破处，销魂雨过，犹恨晴晚。

黄昏把西湖磨成最耀眼的词，
丁香在你的发绺间窃窃私语，窃窃私语，
你眼睛里的鱼游入我的怀中，
我取出一封信，我升上孤山顶眺望你——

岸柳像那祝英台恢复了女儿身，
披一袭青烟的婚纱飘向夜，
你的莲藕心结在水上，你投胎为人，
领我穿过每一处秘闱重阁。

The Sun and Rain of West Lake

The Buddhist relics in the stupa shine at night. During the day
they read the inscription: the ferryman is opening a gate of water!
The once-forbidden inner lake now leaks spring light
with the gift of a brief afternoon play of sun and rain.

From the rippling middle blows the homesick song of silkworms
         and moths –
the sun spits threads in the clouds and weaves nets on the water.
I fish the red carp in your eyes –
come ashore to hold fast this dazzling word.

The lake poets sit and drink up rainbows in the glass.
When wind smokes wave after wave of visitors to sleep,
Su Xiaoxiao comes out of the grave and sings:
where the clouds break, ecstasy after the rain, sigh for the late sun.

Twilight grinds West Lake into the most dazzling word,
lilacs whisper in your tresses, whispering,
the stream of fish in your eyes swims into my arms.
I take out a letter, I rise to the solitary summit to watch you –

like Zhu Yingtai, the willows by the bank put back on their
         maiden clothes
and in a wedding dress of blue smoke, drift to night.
Your lotus heart grows on the water, you reincarnate as a woman
and take me through every pavilion and every secret quarter.

Note: Su Xiaoxiao was a legendary courtesan who lived during the Southern
and Northern Dynasties and was buried by the West Lake. Zhu Yingtai is the
female lead of a Chinese legend of a tragic love story called *The Butterfly
Lovers* (《梁祝》).

城墙与落日
——给朱朱

在自己的土地上漫游是多么不同，
不必为了知识而考古。你和我
走在城墙下。东郊，一间凉亭，
几只鸟，分享了这个重逢的下午。

轩廊外的塔，怀抱箜篌的女人，
秦淮河的泊船隐入六朝的浮华。
从九十九间半房的一个窗口，
太阳的火焰苍白地驶过。

微雨，行人，我注视泥泞的街，
自行车流上空有燕子宛转的口技，
雾的红马轻踏屋顶的蓝瓦，
我沉吟用紫金命名了一座山的人。

湖，倒影波动的形态难以描述，
诗歌一样赤裸，接近于零。
对面的事物互为镜子，交谈的饮者，
伸手触摸的是滚烫的山河。

我用全部的感官呼吸二月，
我品尝南京就像品尝一枚橘子。
回来，风吹衣裳，在日暮的城墙下，
快步走向一树新雨的梅花。

City Walls and Sunset

for Zhu Zhu

How different it is to roam in our own land,
no need of archeology for the mere knowledge. You and I
walk by the city walls. In the eastern suburb, a pavilion,
a few birds, an afternoon shared together, a reunion.

Pagodas seen beyond lofty galleries, a lady holds in her arms an
    ancient harp,
on the Qinhuai River moored boats fade into the fleeting glories of
    six dynasties.
A window from ninety-nine inner chambers,
sunflames pallidly drive through.

Drizzle, passersby, I stare at the muddy street,
above a river of bicycles the ventriloquist swallow turns,
the red horse of fog treads softly on the roof of blue tiles,
I muse on the person who named a mountain Purple Gold.

A lake, wavering patterns of its reflection difficult to describe,
naked like poetry, close to zero.
Opposite things mirror each other, drinkers in a conversation,
rivers and mountains burning close to the touch.

I breathe the second moon of the year with all my organs,
I taste Nanjing as if tasting an orange.
Upon my return, wind through clothes, by the city walls in sunset,
I sprint to a plum tree of blossoms in a fresh rain.

缓缓登上心之山巅

修远——在浓云后面，光
之瀑泻下。井，摇柄如桨，咕噜噜
把渴意泼进瀚海的咽喉、瀚海的眼睛
白杨树，孤零零一棵，承受过天斧

嶙突的路，没有路，只有上下与南北
寥廓惚恍的寂寞。没有虹，只有海市的皮影
一盏油灯点在石窟里。朝圣的躯体褴褛
他灵魂的手杖，丈量着修远

Slow Climb to the Summit of Heart

winding, long – behind thick clouds, the light
cascades. the well, crank like an oar, water grunting
thirst sloshed into the throat and eyes of a vast ocean
a poplar stands alone, a ragged road that has withstood the heavenly

ax, no road, only up and down south and north, wandering
vast loneliness. no rainbow in the sky, only a mirage of shadows
a kerosene lamp lit in the grotto, a pilgrim's body in tatters
the cane of his soul measures this long winding, this journeying

南疆札记

1. 莽荒的上帝读着沙漠的盲文。

2. 库车之夜，我收到火星拍来的电报：这里曾有水的痕迹。

3. 死去的河流像扭曲的干尸，在天空的陈列馆里。

4. 语言，尘埃中的尘埃，在漫漫长路上飞扬。

5. 桨，立在船形棺前。沙海的水手，告诉我，你梦想着什么样
   的航行呢？

6. 商旅的驼队向东，向西，太阳烘烤着眉毛、胡子和馕。

7. 走。一旦躺下，你将冒着被风干的危险。

8. 从看不见的边界到边界，我细数那些消失了的国度。

9. 有一只蚕梦见过罗马，或相反，罗马梦见过一只蚕。

10. 胡杨林里的微风：丝与瓷的谐音。

11. 汉公主刘细君——乌孙国的萨福，嫁给了广袤无边的乡
    愁。

12. 在鸠摩罗什的塑像下，我想到，也许是他晓畅的译文拯救
    了佛教。

13. 前往长安朝觐的三大士，走着与三博士相反的路径。

14. 设若汉武帝知道，汗血马是一种病马，《大宛列传》是否
    将改写？

Notes from South Xinjiang

1. The reckless god reads the braille of the desert.

2. One night in Kuqa, I received a telegram from Mars: there were traces of water.

3. Dead rivers look like twisted mummies in the gallery of the sky.

4. Language, dust of dust, flies on the long, long road.

5. An oar stands before the boat-shaped coffin. Sailors of the desert sea, tell me, what kind of sail do you dream of?

6. Business caravans head east, and west. The sun bakes eyebrows, beards, and crusty flatbreads.

7. Go. Once you lie down, you run the risk of being air-dried.

8. From one invisible border to another, I count those disappeared countries.

9. A silkworm once dreamed of Rome; or rather, Rome once dreamed of a silkworm.

10. Breeze in the dense forest, homonym of silk and porcelain.

11. The Han princess Liu Xijun – Sappho of Wusun country – was married to a vast and endless homesickness.

12. Under the statue of Kumarajiva, I thought: perhaps his intelligible translation saved Buddhism.

13. On their pilgrimage to Chang'an, the three Buddhist masters walked in the opposite direction of the three wise men.

14. If Emperor Wu of the Han dynasty knew that the Ferghana horse was a horse with a disease, would the history of Ferghana be rewritten?

15. 壁画上的供养人有着细细的眉眼。

16. 佛塔——沙漠导航系统。

17. 多么大的遗憾！甘英看见了海，却不知是哪个海。

18. 曼佗罗花瓣——一枚枚五铢钱。

19. 玄奘讲经处的颓垣，升起月牙的耳轮。

20. 在坎儿井的黑暗迷宫里，流水寻找着明媚的葡萄园。

21. 迁徙——从梵语、吐火罗语、回鹘语到汉语；逃过战火和
    千年的遗忘，《弥勒会见记》
    像 凤凰飞入我的视野。

22. 又一首《醉汉木卡姆》：木塞莱斯酒啊，冰冷的美人，快
    浇灭我对你的欲火吧！

23. 在喀什，沈苇对我说：有白杨树的地方就会有人烟。

15. The donors depicted on the murals have thin eyebrows.

16. Stupa – navigation system of the desert.

17. What a pity! Gan Ying saw the sea but did not know which one he saw.

18. Petals of the mandala – one five-baht coin after another.

19. The auricle of the crescent rises on the ruins where Xuanzang preached.

20. In the dark labyrinth of the karez, flowing water looks for bright vineyards.

21. Migration – from Sanskrit to Tocharian, Uighur to Chinese; over battlefields and millennia of forgetting, Maitrisimit flies into my vision like a phoenix.

22. Another Uighur *muqam*: alas the *musailaisi* wine, the ice-cold beauty, come quickly and rub out my burning desire for you!

23. In Kashgar, Shen Wei said to me: there are people wherever poplars grow.

青 海

圆形石堆上扎着经幡，
每一个山顶都戴着相同的王冠，
还有更多的山顶，雪退到了看不见的缝隙中。
火车上的睡眠绵延向可可西里，
一只鸟掉落进沙棘丛，
黄河，泛起胆汁的亮光，
转过一个大湾，流向落日。
几个扛着羊皮筏子的人
瑟瑟路旁，对岸是夜。

Qinghai

a prayer flag rolls around a heap of round stones
every hilltop wears the same crown
there are more hilltops to whose invisible fissures snow
      recedes
slumber on the train meandering toward Hoh Xil
a bird drops into a bush of sandthorns
Yellow River ripples in bilious light
turns around a big bay and flows into sunset
a few souls carry sheepskin rafters
rustling lanes, night on the other shore

腾 冲

火山灰，黑暗如亡灵的记忆，
堆积在那些山的周围。
彝人用它建起村庄，
也用它埋葬死者。

万古的地热烘暖的雪
给油菜花和蜜蜂的脑髓降温。

乘气球的游人只为了一睹大地的伤口。
巨坑边缘明亮，仿佛
匠人打造的一只只陶罐，
里面是圆形虚无。

有过一次爆发，之后
荒芜曾长期统治这地方，
向种子征税，但从未对穿山甲
颁发过大赦令。

银杏树和苦难幸存了下来。

在温泉里洗过澡，
一只矶鹬抖擞着歌喉
跃向天空。屋顶豁地亮了。

Tengchong

volcanic ashes, dark like the memory of dead souls
that pile up around those mountains
that the Yi people use to build villages
and to bury the dead

snow warmed by aeonic geothermals
cools down canola flowers and bee brains

tourists balloon up to inspect the wounds of the earth
immense pits, edges bright, like one
urn after another formed by giants,
hold their circular voids inside

after an outbreak, afterward
bleakness has long reigned in this place
seeds taxed, yet no amnesty order
is issued to pangolins

ginkgo trees and misery survive

after a bath in the hot springs
a thunderbolt bursts out singing
and jolts the sky, out of the blue roofs lit

秋声赋

绵延的小兴安岭，向着俄罗斯
秋天给我一小勺蜜，我把它放回林中
储存在矢车菊的记忆里——
小黑熊晃来晃去到底是为了什么？
垂云扯着秋天大马戏团的帐篷
锣鼓喧天，从五营一路奔向满洲里
静谧，你编织的网可以用来献祭
鄂伦春人，你的鱼皮衣被什么划破了？
老虎避开我们，返回松软的栖息地
虫鸣将给它加冕，在落日金黄的宫殿
树脂什么时候凝成蓝色的琥珀
在腐殖土中，在煤层的锥形塔里
直到在你的脖颈上微微闪光？
松针向左、向右旋转，鬼针草的钩子
潜伏着，等待着一个莽撞的影子
湖的留声机，向田鼠播放一支催眠曲
但它不想睡，它掰开甜苞谷，用尖牙啃着
像一位笨拙的、幸福的隐士
因为爱，透明的、蚂蚱的内翅展开
如雨的拍击声打在细密的叶脉上
我驻足，我倾听，我越过蜘蛛的陷阱
林中，我要拜访的人还没有回来
沉重的松果悬在窗外，装饰着枝头
一个辽金时代的铜马坠子挂在门上
我摇响那铃铛，我惊扰了梅花鹿
并吓跑一群贪吃五味子果的夜鸫
你们，死去的蛾子，一封封夏天的来信

Autumn Whispers

Lesser Khingan meanders, toward Russia
autumn gives me a teaspoonful of honey that I take back
to the woods to hoard in the cornflower's memory –
why does a black bear cub teeter and totter?
Dripping clouds tear at the tent of the autumn circus,
gongs and drums rumble all the way from Wuying to Manchuria.
Dear Quietude, the net you weave could be used as sacrifice.
Dear Oroqens, what has sliced open your fish clothes?
A tiger avoids us and returns to its leafy habitat.
Insect noise crowns it, in the golden sunset palace.
When does the resin cement into blue amber
in the compost, in the conical coal seam
until it glitters around your neck?
Pine needles turn left and right, the hooks of hairy beggar's ticks
ambush a reckless shadow.
The lake gramophone broadcasts a lullaby to a vole
but it does not want to sleep, it peels down the husk and
gnaws on the corn with its sharp teeth like a clumsy happy recluse.
For love, the transparent inner wings of a grasshopper unfold
and beat like rain on the fine veins of a leaf.
I stop, I listen, I cross the spiders' traps
in the woods, the person I want to visit has not yet returned.
Heavy pine cones that hang outside the window grace the branches.
A bronze horse pendant from the Jin dynasty hangs on the door.
I shake the bell, I startle the sika deer,
I scare away a flight of thrushes feasting on magnolia vine berries.
Dear dead moths, like letter after summer letter stuck

贴在玻璃灯罩上，似乎还在往里挤
无人能规劝那一声"啪"里的牺牲
"啪"的诀别，难道一点也不疼？

on the glass shade that still seems to push inward.
No one can call back that "snap" of sacrifice,
that farewell of a "snap," doesn't it ever hurt?

在拉普拉塔河渡船上对另一次旅行的回忆

这水域几乎不能称之为河，它宽得像忘河
一同渡河的人却不一定同归
赫拉克利特感叹过，孔子感叹过
但不容争辩的河流说着它自己的箴言
因为河流乃是大地的舌头
太阳照见船舱里几个爬来爬去的婴儿
城市在一瞥中像一个模糊光斑的恐龙
船尾的人感觉要站得稳些
河流被用来命名逝者，人就只能在岸上
目送、踏歌、深情缅邈地祝福
我想起长江，曾经是界河的另一条河
在镇江和古瓜州之间，在意识的同样
开阔的水域，你和我谈着话
沉思着，试探着将要抵达的对岸
我们的嘴唇贴在了一起

Remembering Another Journey on the La Plata River Ferry

Wide as Lethe, this body of water can barely be called a river.
Those on the same ferry might not return together.
Heraclitus lamented before as did Confucius,
but the indisputable river claims its own precepts,
as a river is a tongue of the earth.
A few babies crawl in the cabin where the sun shines,
a city resembles a mottled dinosaur from a quick glance,
those standing at the stern appreciate the security.
The dead are named after rivers, one is left to stand on the shore
to watch, stomp to songs and bless with deep grief.
I think of the Yangtze, once a border river like La Plata,
between Zhenjiang and ancient Guazhou, in the consciousness
vast as a body of water, you converse with me
and contemplate, in an attempt to reach the other shore.
Then our lips become joined.

3

向后退去的瞬间的大地，
要求成为一个句子，隐匿于一个句子；
要求你带上这个句子继续旅行。

3

The receding world of the moment longs
to be a sentence, to be hidden in a sentence
and asks you to take the sentence along for the trip.

命运与谶
——给师涛

经受了怎样的天罚，这些往昔的诗人。
荷马乞讨于十城，屈原在水上漂，
荷尔德林被阿波罗击中而失语，
尼采（他博学的同胞）借疯子之口喊出
"上帝死了！"，结果死于疯狂。
而林昭，她的名字与命运那可怕的对称，
至今仍在呼唤一场基督降下的雪。

在地上的万国，放逐
贯穿整部人类史，其中诗人的受难
占据显要的一章。正如有人想抹去
"焚尸炉"那一节，代之以"焚烧祭祀"，
有人佯装生活在盛世，秘密信仰着
千年工程，一旦死亡来叩门，
就在名望之环里隐身。

巴黎，礼拜四的雨——巴列霍听见
并说出的，依然在别人的不解中绵绵不绝。
而不远处，策兰飞下米拉波桥，
从一首早已备好的诗中，身轻如燕，
剪碎了万吨泡沫。我们也知道，
"锯开"海子的不是火车，
而是1989那几个神秘的数字。

当又一个诗人从身边被夺走，
哀恸的友人便在他的遗作中挖掘谶，

Providence and Prophecy

for Shi Tao

What divine punishment have they endured, these past poets.
Homer begged his bread on the streets, Qu Yuan floated on the water,
Hölderlin lost his words after being hit by Apollo
and his erudite compatriot Nietzsche cried through the voice of
        a madman,
"God is dead!" and, as a result, died in madness.
As for Lin Zhao, whose name corresponds to her terrifying destiny,
she calls out still for a Christian snow.

In all nations on this planet earth exile
runs through the history of mankind, and that of the suffering poets
occupies a significant chapter. Some want to erase
the section *crematory* and replace it with *burning sacrifice,*
some pretend to be living in the golden age and believe in secret
their thousand-year posterity, once death knocks on the door
they hide themselves in the aura of fame.

Paris, rain on Thursday – what Vallejo heard
and then said meandered despite others' misunderstanding.
Not far off, Celan flew down to Pont Mirabeau,
his body, light like a little sparrow, as if from a prepared poem,
cut through a mass of froth. We all know
what *sliced through* Hai Zi was not the train,
but the mysterious number of 1989.

When another poet was taken away from us,
his mourning friends dug up the prophecy in his works,

仿佛一个命核包裹在话语之壳中：
致命的疏忽源于一次口误。
然而正是在这里，一个事实被放过了：
在客死他乡与等待枪决之间，
未道破的牺牲乃是幸存。

as if the core of life wraps itself in the shell of words:
a slip of the tongue, a fatal negligence.
However it is right here that a fact has been overlooked:
between death in a foreign town and waiting for execution
the unsaid sacrifice is survival.

Note: Lin Zhao's first name, Zhao 昭, means to rehabilitate, prophesying
her posthumous rehabilitation. The 刀 in the character is the radical
for knife, suggesting her martyrdom. In the first line of the last stanza,
"another poet" refers to the late Chinese poet Zhang Zao 张枣.

曼德尔斯塔姆之死

如果他终得以平静自然地死去，
带着没有痛苦的单纯神秘，
让未来的人们不因悲愤而控诉，
而只留连于他诗篇的幻美；
如果加害于他的人不曾抢先一步，
无论以何种巧妙的方式
夺走他黄金的歌喉，
那么，写这首诗的手将不会颤抖。
不！他的死被草率地宣布，
经过改头换面的措辞，
半个世纪以后依然投下阴影，
证实了（如布罗茨基所说）
万有引力的法则——一个黑洞，
全部的人性都将被吸入，
一个人就这样在太阳下失踪。
这并不难，有时间，有地点，
有一部由巨人操作的机器，
纵使钢铁的肋骨也要被勒弯。
让我们记住这可怕的凶年，
在诗人寄居的星球，轰轰烈烈的
时代的马蜂窝已经滚沸，
暴君的拳头进出火星
各地，新的逃亡又开始了。
而这里，天涯的符拉迪沃斯托克，
科里玛半岛附近的一座集中营，
人们关上了门，把他留在床上。
一切正在离他远去，

The Death of Osip Mandelstam

if he died a peaceful natural death
with painless pure mystery
leaving people not to protest in grief
but to linger in the splendor of his poetry
if the assassins were not a step faster
in whichever clever ways
to strip him of his golden singing voice
then the writing hand of this poem would not tremble
no! his death was declared in haste
in rehashed words
and still casts shadows after half a century
and attests (as Joseph Brodsky said)
to the Laws of Gravity – a black hole
into which all humanity is sucked
and a person disappears under the sun
this is yet not difficult, with time and space
with a system operated by a giant
even steel ribs would bend
let us remember the evil age
on a planet where poets dwell, the hornet's nest
of a clamorous age already roils
the fists of a tyrant rub out cinders
everywhere, a new escape begins anew
yet here was Vladivostok on the horizon
in a concentration camp near Kolyma
people shut the door leaving him on the bed
as everything was leaving him

连疼痛也很快要抛弃他，
悲伤不再能抓住他的左心房。
一个被逐者，在帝国版图的
边缘，独自去承担最乖戾的命运，
伸出手触摸想象中的山河，
怀着百感交集的依依不舍。
这个生前没有寸土的人，
死后将得到
                        整个大地的款待。
有什么遗憾？死，已不是什么意外，
现在你竟变得如此亲切，索命者啊！
高高的，他的星座在上空俯瞰这一切，
把最后的火焰吐进他体内，
温暖他冻得麻木的灵魂。
只要一息尚存，他的全部生命
仍将歌唱燃烧的、盛大的星空，
像往昔那样，像一只燕子，
在飞翔的加速度中歌唱。
这星空在1938年的某个冬夜，
朦胧如最后审判的一夜。
淡淡的光，万古不变的光，
垂向莫斯科的一个窗口。
里面一个女人已经睡着，
她脸上的泪水还没有干。
桌上，一封未寄出的信用小楷字
密密麻麻地写满了绝望的爱情：
"是我，娜佳。你在哪儿？永别了！"

even pain would soon renounce him
sorrow no longer groped his left ventricle
a fugitive, on the edge of an empire
alone to bear a most bizarre destiny
hands stretched out to touch the imaginary land
unwillingly with mixed feelings
a man without even a handful of dirt in life
would in death
                    be welcomed by the earth
what to regret? death is no longer a surprise
dear assassins, now shall you become so amicable!
higher up, his constellation watches everything from above
and blows the last flame into his body
to warm his soul that is numb from the cold
even with one last breath his entire being
still sings the vast burning night sky
like before, like a swallow
that sings in the acceleration of flight
the night sky of a winter day in 1938
obscure like the night of Final Judgment
pale light, imperishable light
dripped onto a Moscow window
inside, a lady was already asleep
the tears on her cheeks had not dried
on the table, an unsent letter filled
with small scribbles of despairing love,
"It's me, Nadja. Where are you? So long!"

致米沃什

在你离去的这些年里，
世界依旧是老样子，
只是地球明显地变得不可捉摸，
灾难像惩罚，从天上、地下或海里
降临到人们的餐桌上。
我重读你的诗，你那被逐者的哲人口吻
像来自立陶宛的泉涌，不知疲倦，
那滋养过你的通过你又滋养了别人，
犹如太一生水，水生木，木生火。
而此刻正在燃烧的火，请告诉我
能否诞生一个新的更美的星球？
那里没有秘密警察和住在大脑里的检查制度，
没有破碎的城市①，衰败的乡村，
放下干戈举起船桨的人，
手臂鼓胀着仁慈的力量和美，
游荡在心之山守护的幽谷中。

是的，所有的河流都该流向秩序与财富。
但在我的家乡，它们或变细，
或被拦腰截断，或耻辱地死去，
像在沙漠中风干的蓝蜥蜴。
我不知道，如今你安眠的地方有没有
一条小溪流过，好让你平静地眺望，
好让顺流而下的人能在地图上找到
你赞美过的一片树叶、一颗石子、
或某个妇女脸上翘起的一圈眼睫毛。
你纯洁大度的言辞②让我相信

108

To Czesław Miłosz

In the years after you left,
the world remains the same,
only planet earth becomes elusive,
tribulation like retribution falls on the dining table
from the sky, the earth, and the sea.
As I reread your poems, your philosophical tone
of an outcast, like a wellspring from Lithuania
that tirelessly nourishes you and through you others,
like how Dao creates water, water wood, wood fire.
And the burning fire, please tell me
can you create a brave new planet?
There will be no secret police or censorship in the head,
no *broken city*, declining village,
those who put down arms and pick up oars,
arms beaming in gusto and grace of kindness,
wander in a serene valley guarded by the soul mountain.

Yes, all the rivers should flow into order and wealth.
But in my homeland they either diminish,
are cut at the waist or die in shame,
like blue iguanas air-dried in the desert.
I do not know whether a rivulet flows through
where you rest, so that you could keep watch
in peace, so that those who travel downstream
could find on the map a leaf, a stone
or the tipped eyelashes of some lady you praised.
Your *pure and generous words* make me believe

在你想象的至福国度里，没有一条河流会消逝。
其中最神奇的一条：阿尔菲河，
据说，消失在大海之后
又在另一块陆地上再度涌现。
你的声音也是这样，穿过暗夜，
在不可预料之岸激起了久久的回响。

注：①②均引自米沃什的诗
2011/6/29 米沃什百年诞辰前日

in the blessed kingdom you imagined, not a river disappears.
The most magical one – the river Alpheus –
is said to flow into another continent
after disappearing in the ocean.
So does your voice that crosses dark nights
lapping on an unknown shore, resounding lastingly.

Note: written on June 29, 2011, before Czesław Miłosz's centennial,
words in italics are quotes from Miłosz.

送别C.D.Wright

写作，一个向晚的词
在黑键盘上徘徊
也许耗尽余生，幸运之光
终会从密不透风的毛细血管筛下
照见你幽暗的心脏
那里，另一个姐妹星团已向西倾斜
那七颗亮星彷佛七堆篝火
还未燃尽
想象力这真理的皇后——
如波德莱尔所说，将为你戴上
阿肯色州的绿松石耳坠
并且对自己的杰作感到满意
乌鸦还会在你莳弄过的花园里唱歌
因为新雪使它高兴，因为那
虚构的皇后逃了
你躲在萱草丛中
为煮在偷渡客铁锅里的土豆
而高兴，当落日
又一次拜访了坡地上的
无名死者

Farewell to C. D. Wright

writing, a twilight word
lingers on the black keyboard
perhaps after exhausting the remaining years
the fortunate light will eventually pierce
your gloomy heart through airtight capillaries
there another Pleiades already slants westward
seven stars, like seven bonfires
have not died out
imagination, the queen of truth—
as Baudelaire said, would put on
turquoise earrings from Arkansas for you
and be satisfied with its own masterpiece
a blackbird still sings in your trimmed garden
as it delights in the new snow, as
the fictional queen flees
you hide in the shrubbery
and feel happy for the potatoes
that are boiling in the refugees' wok
when the setting sun visits
again on the slope
the nameless dead

双行体

1

被翻越的多雪的山脊，无名死者丰饶的夜航，
白桦树燃起多枝烛台，黎明洗劫了杜鹃花之梦。

2

在我的耳朵里撞钟，你发明的那截断众流的句子，
汩汩注入国家那消音器一般的葫芦。

3

一个发不出声音的东西的回声，像一个被脐带
绞杀的词，在寂静的子宫里，震耳欲聋。

4

火狐嗅着雪，兜更大的圈子，它不知道词语为何物，
但它知道雪的味道远胜过人类谎言的口香糖。

Couplets

1

snowy ridges crossed, lavish night sails of the nameless dead
white birches light up candelabras, dawn rifles azalea dreams

2

tolling the bell in my ears, your invented sentences subvert
      the mainstream
and flood into the nation's silencer, a gourd

3

an echo of a thing that makes no sound, as a word strangled
by the umbilical cord, in the still of the womb, deafens the ear

4

a red fox sniffs the snow, detours further, not knowing what a word is,
it knows the smell of snow beats by far the chewing gum of human lies

5

郊区破碎，如遭雷击。三个隐形人潜伏在洗足店门外。
突然，说辞笨拙——摄像头坏了。

6

在他展出的折磨肉体的器具中，避孕套（来自一个被强暴
但无权生育的妇女），像一根阴茎萎缩在塑料袋里。

7

将我的注意力从诗歌引开的东西戴着迷人的面具，
而那面具的后面站着广阔的无名。

8

飞碟云，放着光。给它足够的信号，足够的友善，
几个摇晃着巨颅的影子就会下来，为地球送来灵魂。

5

suburbs in pieces, as if struck by thunder. three invisible men lurk
     outside a pedicure shop
out of the blue, out of words – the CCTV goes out of order

6

among the torture gadgets that he displays, a condom (from a
     raped woman
stripped of her right to give birth) curls like a penis in a plastic bag

7

the thing that distracts me from poetry wears a charming mask
and behind the mask stands the vast namelessness

8

a UFO cloud emits light. with ample signal enough empathy a
     few shadows
that shake their giant heads will come down and send souls to
     the earth

9

我看见那个墓道般的入口了，我猜想那里面将比
但丁的地狱更黑更深，且已经人满为患。

10

这张床大如北方，带着我漂流，好客的鬼魂夜里出来，
用哗哗的水声催我入眠，温暖如冰灯，我睡着了。

11

告诉我，在公众事件中始终不吭一声的同行，
是否从被抛弃的多数人那里赎回了本属于你的权力？

12

恐惧——断头台的遗产，被沉默继承了下来，
我听说沉默家族人丁兴旺，日日以眼泪为粮食。

9

I see the entrance to the grave, I figure inside it will be
darker and deeper than Dante's Inferno and already overpopulated

10

this bed, big as the North, takes me along adrift, hospitable ghosts
        come out of night
and hush me to sleep by the rush of water, warm as an ice lamp, I
        fall asleep

11

tell me, dear colleagues, you who keep silent forever at public events
have you redeemed the power you deserve from the deserted masses?

12

fear – legacy from the guillotine, is inherited by silence
I hear the family of silence is prospering and day by day takes tears
        for food

13

历史的循环诡计：我们会老去，僵尸却不会老。
看吧，半个世纪过去了，僵尸竟然又活了过来！

14

误入一个不受欢迎的聚会，仿佛跻身于饕餮鬼的宴席，
我需要的是赶走苍蝇，我没有兴趣看它怎样作揖。

15

越挖越深的极权主义的矿井只通向坍塌。
记忆黑如煤晶，光从你躯体的筛孔缓缓漏下。

16

黄昏，枯坐在山坡上。天空百科全书向我打开：
每一页都写着血红，血红，血红。

13

the circular trick of history: we will grow old, zombies will not,
watch out, after half a century zombies come back to life again!

14

walking into an unwelcoming party, as if arrayed in a feast for
        the gluttons
I need to shoo away the fly, I have no interest in seeing it bow its back

15

dug deeper, the totalitarian mines only lead to collapse
memory black like coal crystals, light leaks from the sieve of
        your body

16

at twilight, sitting emaciated on the slope. encyclopedia of the sky
        opens to me:
on every page the nibs blood red, blood red, blood red

17

在9·11纪念馆的地下层，数千张死者的脸一齐凝视着我，
仿佛我们置身于同一条船的底舱，而上面是阳光和平静的生活。

18

不确定性：我们这个时代的魅影，
仿佛吹着水泡但从不露面的尼斯湖的怪物。

19

一个梦：被监测到的独裁者的基因图谱，在禁止
公开的档案里，用密码和隐形墨水写成。

20

他已学会在水面上刻字，他已学会用石头的冷眼瞧我们，
这襁褓里的飞毛腿，几乎已追上了永恒。

17

in the basement of the 9/11 Memorial, thousands of dead faces stare
    at me in unison
as if we were at the bottom of the same boat, facing sunlight and
    a life in peace

18

uncertainty: the phantom of our age
is like the Loch Ness Monster that blows bubbles yet never appears

19

a dream: the detected gene map of the dictator, in the confidential
files, written in codes and invisible ink

20

he has learned to etch words on the water's surface. he has learned
    to look us up
with stone-cold eyes. the swaddled fast runner nearly catches up
    with infinity

21

一页桨，横过暗礁掀起的千层幕墙，在恶鲨的牙齿
和灯塔的眺望之间，摆渡太阳。

22

长久地忍受一个词的磨难，直到它把你吐出，
像一个硬核，在墓穴里发芽。

23

石头不会自行挪动，暴露出压在它下面的阴影，
除非找到另一块石头，另一个支点。

24

如果你见过两只鸊鹈在水上跳起的爱之舞，
你就理解了什么是宇宙的同步性。

25

那陨落的，借我们的手捧起，又从指缝间漏下，
这些曾经是星星的，眼泪一样滚烫的沙粒。

21

a paddle, across a thousand curtain walls thrust by hidden reefs
between sharks' teeth and the watch of a lighthouse, ferries the sun

22

to endure the tribulation of a word, until it spits you out
like a hard core that sprouts in a grave

23

a stone does not flit by itself, exposing the shadow crushed under it
unless there is another stone, another fulcrum

24

if you have seen the courtship dance of two grebes on the water
you will understand the synchronicity of the universe

25

the fallen, lifted by our hands, leaking through our fingers, are the sands
that once belonged to the stars and are now seething like tears

来自基弗的画

是的，这是大地的真实写照。
生活模仿了艺术——废墟如记忆
在大脑深处燃烧着。太多的灾难，
非自然的，道德的，语言的，
我们已经习惯。在一个火山口般的大坑边缘
喝茶，造爱，乘电梯做穿越地狱的旅行，
瑟瑟的风彷佛死神温柔的祝福。
太多隐忍，当城管暴打一个小摊贩；
女中学生被自己的同伴当街羞辱，
围观者看见的只是被斗败的蟋蟀。
人心滑向深渊而股市崩盘。
氰化钠爆炸，在第二个广岛，
在大阅兵即将开始的闷热的八月，
彷佛冬眠的战神突然醒来。
冲击波的威力（我们曾在文革期间的
核战宣传片中见过）摧枯拉朽，
回眸间，那喷火女怪的舌头已舔破
疲惫如居民楼玻璃窗的梦境。
银灰的金属流体美如虚拟的液态人，
正匍匐前进，去吞噬消防员年轻的肉身。
其中一位，刚尝了口新婚之蜜，
旋即化作灿烂的火雨。
是的，生活模仿了艺术，但技法笨拙，
废墟的签名永远是：一片狼藉。
烧成骷髅的汽车的空架子
组成兵马俑的方阵，浩浩荡荡，
等待着被检阅，而蒲公英的小降落伞

From the Paintings by Anselm Kiefer

Yes, this is the true picture of the earth.
Life mimics art – ruins burn
like memory deep in the mind. We are used
to the many catastrophes that are unnatural, moral
or linguistic. On the edge of a volcanic pit
we drink tea, make love, take a life through purgatory,
wind whistles the gentle blessing of death.
Too much forbearance, when an urban management officer
beats a street vendor; or when a middle school student
is humiliated by her peers, bystanders see her only as a defeated cricket.
Morality slides toward the abyss and the stock market crashes.
Sodium cyanide explodes in another Hiroshima
in the sultry August before the Military Parade is about to begin,
as if the warlord is suddenly awake.
The power of shockwaves all-powerful, (as we saw
in the nuclear war videos of the Cultural Revolution),
in the blink of an eye, the tongue of the fire-spitting monstress
licks through the exhausted dreams of residential building windows.
Beautiful like a liquid being, silver-gray metal flows
and winds forward to swallow the firefighters' flesh.
One among them, who has just tasted the honey of marriage,
soon turns into brilliant rains of fire.
Yes, life mimics art, yet, in its clumsy way,
the signature of ruins remains: a mess.
Skeletons of burned cars
form a terracotta phalanx, massive and mighty,
awaited is the review. Meanwhile the little parachutes of dandelions

载着失踪者的名字漂浮到了海上。
农民工的棚子早已不知去向。
一只收音机反复在唱：
明天，亲爱的妈妈将找到我的骨头。
我们果真能熬到天亮吗？
果真有讳莫如深的人指给我们看，
一条穿越秘而不宣的设计图，
实际并不存在的防线吗？
官方忙于辟谣，疯子在赶写赞歌，
我们闻所未闻的真相在黑暗中酣睡着。
一个窗前的小女孩被壮丽的蘑菇云惊呆，
她张大了嘴，像苏拉密站在焚尸炉外。

drift to the sea with the names of the disappeared.

The workers' sheds are nowhere to be found.

A radio repeats:

tomorrow, *my dear mother will find my bones.*

Can we really stand until dawn?

In fact, an anonymous man points out to us

a secret route out,

would there be no defense on the way?

Authorities are burying the rumors, madmen are writing praise songs,

the truth that we will never know sleeps and snores in the dark.

A girl by the window has her mouth wide open, shocked

by the magnificent mushroom clouds, as if a Sulamith before

> the crematorium.

语言简史

既无名称亦无目光，从未有过酣畅淋漓的流动
——冰川宝蓝色的沉睡。寒冬严峻的刻刀
在那透明的棺椁表面继续跳着透明的死亡舞蹈。

语言抵达那片缓坡，在昨天的猛犸离去之后。
那边走来一个穿桦皮衣的人，他有着从地狱归来的
但丁一样苍白的面容。他缓缓吐出一个词——"花"。

A Brief History of Language

not a name not a line of sight, never a thorough run of water
—slumbers of the turquoise icebergs. a severe wintry engraver
dances still a transparent dance of death on the transparent
      coffin surface.

arrival of language at that soft slope, after yesterday's mammoths left.
there comes a man in a birch-bark coat, wearing a Dantesque pale face
as if returning from the netherworld. slowly he blurts a word out
      —"flower."

在纽约上州乡间的一次散步
——给李栋

枫叶的火正旺，要不了几天将转暗
熄灭于远近每一座小山迎来的雪
但这里的晚秋将比我逗留得更久些
它没有路要赶，不需要回到
一个火热而盲目的国度
我来，恰逢其时，带着东方人的狡黠和好奇
眼睛接受着晚霞好客的款待
且不必拘泥于这片风景的属性
天气把我的好心情放大三倍
一些房子位于山顶，占据更远的视野
另一些散落于林间和路旁
围着与习俗、等级相似的篱笆
私人领地的告示引导我学会绕着道走
我足够机敏，但鹿群更令我羡慕
后蹄轻轻一弹，自由游荡在整个地区
或就近研究人类古怪的习性
峡谷的大型音箱不播放音乐而播放静谧
天空如此繁忙，如百老汇的剧院
不时地，一架私人飞机的引擎
像一根点燃的火柴穿越客厅消失于厨房后门外
那里的小池塘顿时烟雾弥漫
草地连着灌木丛，乌鸦像一群女巫
翩然而降，并秘密交换了新的咒语
（这一次我毫不在意它们叫喊的次数）
天色渐暗，一闪一闪的车灯在询问：

A Walk in Upstate New York Country

for Dong Li

The maples are burning and in a few days will dim
and die out in the snow that is embraced by every hill
from near and far, but late autumn will stay longer than I will.
It does not have to scurry on its journey, or return
to a blind and frantic nation.
I come at the right time, with the cunning and curiosity of an
        oriental man.
Evening hues color my eyes with their hospitality
and open them to landscapes unlike this one.
The weather magnifies my good mood three times more.
Some houses sit atop the hill with a farther outlook,
others scatter in the woods or by the road,
fenced up according to custom and social status.
Notices of private property lead me to make a detour.
I am alert but even more so I am envious of the deer herd.
A gentle kick of their hind legs, and they are free to wander in the area
or take the opportunity to study the odd behaviors of mankind.
The loudspeakers of the valley play no music but stillness.
In a sky busy as Broadway,
from time to time a private jet flits past
as if a burning match runs through the living and disappears behind
        the kitchen.
The little pond suddenly turns smoggy.
Shrubberies lean on grasses. Like witches,
a flight of crows descends softly and exchanges their new mantras
        in secret.
(This time around, I do not care how much they scream.)

你迷路了吗？需要载你一程吗？
谢谢，我只是走得稍远了一些
为了与摇晃在桌前的旧我拉开点距离
但大雁不存在诸如此类的想法
脖颈前伸着紧贴树梢飞过，翅膀彷佛
赛龙舟水手的桨叶，整齐地举落
它们扔下问候，我也礼貌地回应了它们
挥手间，那歌唱的人字型已穿过满月

The sky darkening, headlights of cars flash and seem to ask:
are you lost? Do you need a ride?
No, thank you, I am just walking a little farther
to stretch the distance from the old I before the shaking desk.
But the wild geese have no such thoughts.
Neck forward, they fly close to the treetops and their wings,
like the oars of a dragon-boat paddler, beat evenly up and down.
They drop their greetings and I politely answer them.
In the wave of a hand, their V-formations are singing across
        the full moon.

Acknowledgments

Gratitude to a grant from the PEN/Heim Translation Fund and a joint residency at OMI Ledig House. Our sincere thanks to Giramondo and to Will, David, and the whole Deep Vellum team. Many thanks to the editors and readers of the magazines in which these translations or their earlier versions first appeared:

Arkansas International: "A Walk Down Montmartre," "Autumn Whispers"

Asia Literary Review: "Forgetting," "Jiaocheng, 1970," "The Sun and Rain of West Lake," "Notes from South Xinjiang"

Asymptote: "untitled"

Bennington Review: "Remembering Another Journey on the La Plata River Ferry"

Blackbird: "Providence and Prophecy," "The Death of Osip Mandelstam," "Tower of Enchantment"

Brooklyn Rail: "*from* Death and Praise," "The Circus," "Couplets"

Gulf Coast: "*from* Fragments and Farewell Songs"

Kenyon Review: "Farewell to C. D. Wright"

Lana Turner: "The Gleaner Song," "Max Ernst," "Jorge Luis Borges Imagines China"

Michigan Quarterly Review: "Bois de Boulogne," "To Czesław Miłosz"

PEN America: "Paul Celan by the Seine," "Near," "Metaphor of the Floating Life," "City Walls and Sunset," "Slow Climb to the Summit of Heart," "A Brief History of Language" with Translator's Note

Pathlight: "Q&A," "From the Paintings by Anselm Kiefer," "A Walk in Upstate New York Country"

Plume: "Qinghai," "Tengchong"

The poem "Near" and the introductory note "The World Migrating: On Translating Song Lin" were reprinted in *Australian Poetry*.

About the Author and Translator

SONG Lin is one of the most distinctive poets from the People's Republic of China. The author of numerous books of poetry, poetry anthologies, and prose, he has had two previous collections, *Fragments and Farewell Songs* and *City Walls and Sunset,* published bilingually in France. He is the poetry editor of the journal *Jintian* [*Today*]. Among his honors are fellowships from the Netherlands, Romania, and Hong Kong, as well as the Shanghai, Dong Dang Zi, and Chang Yao Literature Prizes. He has held residencies at OMI Ledig House Translation Lab and Vermont Studio Center.

Dong LI is a multilingual author who translates from Chinese, English, French, and German. He is the English translator of *The Wild Great Wall* (Phoneme Media, 2018) by the Chinese poet Zhu Zhu, the German cotranslator (with Lea Schneider) of *Gesellschaft für Flugversuche* (Carl Hanser Verlag, 2019) by the Chinese poet Zang Di, and the Chinese translator of 《相伴》 *Be With* (East China Normal University Press, 2021) by the American poet Forrest Gander. For his own literary projects, he has received fellowships from Akademie Schloss Solitude, the Camargo and Humboldt Foundations, and Yaddo. As a translator, he has received support from a PEN/Heim Translation Fund Grant, Ledig House, Henry Luce Foundation/Vermont Studio Center, and the American Literary Translators Association.

Thank you all
for your support.
We do this for you,
and could not do
it without you.

PARTNERS

pixel ||| texel

EMBREY FAMILY
FOUNDATION

ALLRED
CAPITAL MANAGEMENT
of
RAYMOND JAMES®

ADDITIONAL DONORS, CONT'D

Mark Haber
Mary Cline
Maynard Thomson
Michael Reklis
Mike Soto
Mokhtar Ramadan
Nikki & Dennis Gibson
Patrick Kukucka
Patrick Kutcher
Rev. Elizabeth & Neil Moseley
Richard Meyer

Scott & Katy Nimmons
Sherry Perry
Sydneyann Binion
Stephen Harding
Stephen Williamson
Susan Carp
Susan Ernst
Theater Jones
Tim Perttula
Tony Thomson

SUBSCRIBERS

Ned Russin
Michael Binkley
Michael Schneiderman
Aviya Kushner
Kenneth McClain
Eugenie Cha
Stephen Fuller
Joseph Rebella
Brian Matthew Kim

Anthony Brown
Michael Lighty
Erin Kubatzky
Shelby Vincent
Margaret Terwey
Ben Fountain
Caroline West
Ryan Todd
Gina Rios

Caitlin Jans
Ian Robinson
Elena Rush
Courtney Sheedy
Elif Ağanoğlu
Laura Gee
Valerie Boyd
Brian Bell

AVAILABLE NOW FROM DEEP VELLUM

MICHÈLE AUDIN · *One Hundred Twenty-One Days* · translated by Christiana Hills · FRANCE

BAE SUAH · *Recitation* · translated by Deborah Smith · SOUTH KOREA

MARIO BELLATIN · *Mrs. Murakami's Garden* · translated by Heather Cleary · MEXICO

EDUARDO BERTI · *The Imagined Land* · translated by Charlotte Coombe · ARGENTINA

CARMEN BOULLOSA · *Texas: The Great Theft* · *Before* · *Heavens on Earth*
translated by Samantha Schnee · Peter Bush · Shelby Vincent · MEXICO

MAGDA CARNECI · *FEM* · translated by Sean Cotter · ROMANIA

LEILA S. CHUDORI · *Home* · translated by John H. McGlynn · INDONESIA

MATHILDE CLARK · *Lone Star* · translated by Martin Aitken · DENMARK

SARAH CLEAVE, ed. · *Banthology: Stories from Banned Nations* ·
IRAN, IRAQ, LIBYA, SOMALIA, SUDAN, SYRIA & YEMEN

LOGEN CURE · *Welcome to Midland: Poems* · USA

ANANDA DEVI · *Eve Out of Her Ruins* · translated by Jeffrey Zuckerman · MAURITIUS

PETER DIMOCK · *Daybook from Sheep Meadow* · USA

CLAUDIA ULLOA DONOSO · *Little Bird*, translated by Lily Meyer · PERU/NORWAY

ROSS FARRAR · *Ross Sings Cheree & the Animated Dark: Poems* · USA

ALISA GANIEVA · *Bride and Groom* · *The Mountain and the Wall*
translated by Carol Apollonio · RUSSIA

FERNANDA GARCIA LAU · *Out of the Cage* · translated by Will Vanderhyden · ARGENTINA

ANNE GARRÉTA · *Sphinx* · *Not One Day* · *In/concrete* · translated by Emma Ramadan · FRANCE

JÓN GNARR · *The Indian* · *The Pirate* · *The Outlaw* · translated by Lytton Smith · ICELAND

GOETHE · *The Golden Goblet: Selected Poems* · *Faust, Part One*
translated by Zsuzsanna Ozsváth and Frederick Turner · GERMANY

NOEMI JAFFE · *What are the Blind Men Dreaming?* · translated by Julia Sanches & Ellen Elias-Bursac · BRAZIL

CLAUDIA SALAZAR JIMÉNEZ · *Blood of the Dawn* · translated by Elizabeth Bryer · PERU

PERGENTINO JOSÉ · *Red Ants* · MEXICO

TAISIA KITAISKAIA · *The Nightgown & Other Poems* · USA

JUNG YOUNG MOON · *Seven Samurai Swept Away in a River* · *Vaseline Buddha*
translated by Yewon Jung · SOUTH KOREA

KIM YIDEUM · *Blood Sisters* · translated by Ji yoon Lee · SOUTH KOREA

JOSEFINE KLOUGART · *Of Darkness* · translated by Martin Aitken · DENMARK

YANICK LAHENS · *Moonbath* · translated by Emily Gogolak · HAITI

FORTHCOMING FROM DEEP VELLUM

SHANE ANDERSON · *After the Oracle* · USA

MARIO BELLATIN · *Beauty Salon* · translated by David Shook · MEXICO

MIRCEA CĂRTĂRESCU · *Solenoid*
translated by Sean Cotter · ROMANIA

LEYLÂ ERBIL · *A Strange Woman*
translated by Nermin Menemencioğlu & Amy Marie Spangler· TURKEY

RADNA FABIAS · *Habitus* · translated by David Colmer · CURAÇAO/NETHERLANDS

SARA GOUDARZI · *The Almond in the Apricot* · USA

GYULA JENEI · *Always Different* · translated by Diana Senechal · HUNGARY

UZMA ASLAM KHAN • *The Miraculous True History of Nomi Ali* • PAKISTAN

SONG LIN · *The Gleaner Song: Selected Poems* · translated by Dong Li · CHINA

TEDI LÓPEZ MILLS · *The Book of Explanations* · translated by Robin Myers · MEXICO

JUNG YOUNG MOON · *Arriving in a Thick Fog*
translated by Mah Eunji and Jeffrey Karvonen · SOUTH KOREA

FISTON MWANZA MUJILA · *The Villain's Dance,* translated by Roland Glasser · *The River in the Belly:
Selected Poems,* translated by Bret Maney · DEMOCRATIC REPUBLIC OF CONGO

LUDMILLA PETRUSHEVSKAYA · *Kidnapped: A Crime Story,* translated by Marian Schwartz · *The New
Adventures of Helen: Magical Tales,* translated by Jane Bugaeva · RUSSIA

SERGIO PITOL · *The Love Parade* · translated by G. B. Henson · MEXICO

MANON STEFAN ROS · *The Blue Book of Nebo* · WALES

JIM SCHUTZE · *The Accommodation* · USA

SOPHIA TERAZAWA · *Winter Phoenix: Testimonies in Verse* · POLAND

BOB TRAMMELL · *Jack Ruby & the Origins of the Avant-Garde in Dallas & Other Stories* · USA

BENJAMIN VILLEGAS · *ELPASO: A Punk Story* · translated by Jay Noden · MEXICO